HE MEANT YOU TO BE YOU

J. J. LeVan

Illustrated by James Newton

Copyright Notice
He Meant You to be You

First edition. Copyright © 2023 by J. J. LeVan. The information contained in this book is the intellectual property of J. J. LeVan and is governed by United States and International copyright laws. All rights reserved. No part of this publication, either text or image, may be used for any purpose other than personal use. Therefore, reproduction, modification, storage in a retrieval system, or retransmission, in any form or by any means, electronic, mechanical, or otherwise, for reasons other than personal use, except for brief quotations for reviews or articles and promotions, is strictly prohibited without prior written permission by the publisher.

This is a work of fiction. Names, characters, businesses, places, events, locales, and incidents are either the products of the author's imagination or used in a fictitious manner. Any resemblance to actual persons, living or dead, or actual events is purely coincidental.

Scripture taken from the International Children's Bible®. Copyright © 1986, 1988, 1999 by Thomas Nelson. Used by permission. All rights reserved.

Cover and Interior Design: James Newton, Derinda Babcock
Editor(s): Derinda Babcock, Donna Wyland, Deb Haggerty

PUBLISHED BY: Elk Lake Publishing, Inc., 35 Dogwood Drive, Plymouth, MA 02360, 2023
_____

Library Cataloging Data
Names: LeVan, J. J. (J. J. LeVan)
He Meant You to be You / J. J. LeVan
42 p. 21.6 cm × 21.6 cm (8.5 in × 8.5 in.)
ISBN-13: 978-1-64949-943-1 (paperback) | 978-1-64949-941-7 (trade hardcover) | 978-1-64949-942-4 (trade paperback) | 978-1-64949-940-0 (e-book)
Key Words: God Autism Picture Book; Christian Autism; Books for Autistic Children; Autism Bedtime Picture Book; Picture Book about God; Special Need Picture Book; Bedtime Books for Autistic Girls
Library of Congress Control Number: 2023945406

Author Dedication

Blake,

God meant you to be the wonderful person that you are.

You have taught me far more than I could ever teach you.

Love, Mom

God gave a special gift to us.
I think it's plain to see.
He made you special EVERY WAY,
Especially to me.

I hope you know I love you so.
God loves you even MORE.
We need to talk about HIS love.
There's so much to explore.

God loves you in the morning time
And sees you in your bed.
He helps you to be brave and strong
To face the day ahead.

God loves your finger fidget fun
And knows you don't like change.
He loves your fancy schedule chart
So days don't seem so strange.

God loves your helpful therapist,
The one with squishy clay.
He knows the toys she hides inside
And loves to see you play.

God loves your jumping up and down
And when you swing up high.
He sees your pointing picture class
And hears you when you cry.

God loves you if the noise is LOUD
And loves you if it's not.
He sees you when you spin around
And get so very hot.

God loves you when you flap your hands
And when you plug your ears.
He loves your French fries in the car
And knows your foodie fears.

God loves your really cool new shades
And your new shady hat.
He loves the way you sing your tunes
And how you copycat.

God loves your eyes that move about
And look up to the sky.
He sees what you are looking at
And doesn't wonder why.

God's love is with you everywhere
And with you every day.
But, if that's hard to think about,
It's probably okay.